The Geology Of The Country Around Eastbourne

Clement Reid

In the interest of creating a more extensive selection of rare historical book reprints, we have chosen to reproduce this title even though it may possibly have occasional imperfections such as missing and blurred pages, missing text, poor pictures, markings, dark backgrounds and other reproduction issues beyond our control. Because this work is culturally important, we have made it available as a part of our commitment to protecting, preserving and promoting the world's literature. Thank you for your understanding.

334.

MEMOIRS OF THE GEOLOGICAL SURVEY.

ENGLAND AND WALES.

THE GEOLOGY OF
THE COUNTRY AROUND
EASTBOURNE.

(EXPLANATION OF SHEET 334.)

BY

CLEMENT REID, F.L.S., F.G.S.

PUBLISHED BY ORDER OF THE LORDS COMMISSIONERS OF HER MAJESTY'S TREASURY.

LONDON:
PRINTED FOR HER MAJESTY'S STATIONERY OFFICE,
BY WYMAN & SONS, LIMITED, FETTER LANE, E.C.

And to be purchased, either directly or through any Bookseller, from
EYRE AND SPOTTISWOODE, EAST HARDING STREET, FLEET STREET, E.C., and
32, ABINGDON STREET, WESTMINSTER, S.W.; or
JOHN MENZIES & Co., 12, HANOVER STREET, EDINBURGH, and
90, WEST NILE STREET, GLASGOW; or
HODGES, FIGGIS, & Co., LIMITED, 104, GRAFTON STREET, DUBLIN.

1898.

Price Sixpence.

PREFACE.

The ground described in the following pages includes a length of about 20 miles of the coast of Sussex, in which Beachy Head, Eastbourne, Newhaven, and Seaford are the chief places. It is contained in Sheet 334 of the New Series of the Geological Survey Map of England and Wales.

This part of the country was long ago brought to the notice of geologists, especially by Mantell and Dixon, who gave an account of the strata with illustrations of their fossil contents. Topley, in the Geological Survey Memoir on the Geology of the Weald (pp. 158, 159), supplied additional information, and made reference to the writings of previous observers. The Chalk cliffs between Seaford and Eastbourne have subsequently been described by Mr. Whitaker in further detail. The zonal subdivisions of the Chalk, first indicated in this district by Dr. Barrois, have since been more fully worked out by several zealous observers.

The district to which the present pamphlet is an explanation was originally mapped for the Geological Survey by the late H. W. Bristow (in Sheet 5 of the Old Series, 1864), but the superficial deposits were not then represented. During the general revision of the Geological Survey Maps of the South of England the ground was re-examined by Mr. W. A. E. Ussher, who in 1884 mapped the superficial deposits on the New Series 1-inch Map, the Secondary rocks being afterwards re-surveyed by Mr. Clement Reid on the 6-inch scale in the years 1889 and 1890. A complete series of these 6-inch maps has been made and deposited in the Office for public reference.

The present Explanation has been prepared by Mr. Reid. It is intended only as a general guide to the use of the Map, until a more detailed account of the whole surrounding region can be issued. The Cretaceous rocks will be more fully described in a monograph on the Upper Cretaceous Formations, by Mr. Jukes-Browne, now in preparation.

This part of the Sussex coast is a favourite residential district, more noted for its healthiness than for its mineral wealth. The applications of geology, therefore, are there mainly such as bear on the desirability of building-sites, materials for building, and water-supply. Minerals for use outside the district are almost unknown.

ARCH. GEIKIE
Director-General.

Geological Survey Office,
28, Jermyn Street, London, S.W.
5th July, 1898.

CONTENTS.

	page
Preface by the Director-General	iii
Introduction	1
Weald Clay	2
Lower Greensand	3
Gault	3
Upper Greensand	4
Chalk	5
Woolwich Beds and London Clay	8
Clay with Flints	10
Valley Gravel or Coombe Rock	10
Alluvium and Shingle	10
Disturbances and Surface Erosion	11
Water Supply and Economics	13

ILLUSTRATIONS.

Fig. 1. Pecten asper, Lam.,
„ 2. Exogyra conica, Sow., } Fossils of the Upper Greensand — 4
„ 3. Vermicularia concava, Sow.,

„ 4. Ammonites rotomagensis, Brong.,
„ 5. ———— varians, Sow., } Fossils of the Lower Chalk — 6
„ 6. Scaphites æqualis, Sow.,

„ 7. Echinoconus subrotundus, Mant.,
„ 8. Terebratulina gracilis, Schloth.,
„ 9. Holaster planus, Mant., } Fossils of the Middle Chalk — 7
„ 10. Inoceramus mytiloides, Mant.,
„ 11. Rhynchonella Cuvieri, d'Orb.,

„ 12. Micraster coranguinum, Leske.,
„ 13. Marsupites ornatus, Miller,
„ 14. Rhynchonella plicatilis (var. octoplicata), Sow., } Fossils of the Upper Chalk — 8
„ 15. Echinocorys vulgaris, Bregnius,

„ 16. Ostrea Bellovacina, Lam.,
„ 17. Cyrena cuneiformis, Sow., } Fossils of the Woolwich Beds — 9
„ 18. Melania inquinata, Defr.,

Map of part of the Foreshore near Beachy Head — 12

THE GEOLOGY OF

THE COUNTRY AROUND

EASTBOURNE.

INTRODUCTION.

SHEET 334 of the Geological Survey Map takes in an area of 45 square miles in Sussex, including the eastern termination of the South Downs and the coast from Eastbourne to Seaford and Newhaven. The whole of this country, except the alluvial flats and a small spread of low ground north of Eastbourne, consists of undulating Downs, with a bold escarpment facing east-north-east, vertical sea-cliffs facing south, and intricate winding valleys, now quite dry. Willingdon Hill reaches a height of 665 feet, and at a few other points heights of 600 feet are attained; but most of these Downs are of considerably lower elevation, the highest cliff at Beachy Head being 525 feet. Two tidal estuaries break the line of vertical Chalk cliffs. That of the Ouse forms the harbour at Newhaven, and is navigable for a considerable distance inland; that of the Cuckmere is much smaller, and is now almost blocked by a bar of shingle. North of Eastbourne the large alluvial flat, known as Willingdon Level, would often be flooded at spring-tides were it not for the enormous accumulation of shingle-beach which forms Langney Point. An attempt will be made in the following pages to explain the meaning of these various features.

The formations represented on Sheet 334 are the following:—

Recent	Shingle. Alluvium.
Pleistocene	Valley Gravel. Clay with Flints.
Eocene	London Clay. Woolwich Beds.
Upper Cretaceous	Upper Chalk. Middle Chalk. Lower Chalk. Upper Greensand. Gault.
Lower Cretaceous	Lower Greensand. Weald Clay.

The successive outcrops of these formations when traced on the Map show that the area belongs to the southward slope of the great Wealden anticline, where this anticline is passing into the Tertiary syncline of the Hampshire Basin. Most of this syncline, however, is here beneath the sea, and the abrupt change of strike which takes place between Eastbourne and Beachy Head suggests that we may there have reached its eastern limit.

Little of the land is of much agricultural value, great part of it being in the state of rough pasture, either alluvial meadow or open Chalk Down. The large extent of the open downs is one of the principal attractions of the district; the Chalk slopes being famed also for their healthiness and the perfect dryness of the houses built on them. During the late autumn and winter months the higher Downs are, however, often capped with low clouds, the condensation from which supplies numerous dew-ponds. It should not be forgotten, therefore, that there may be a considerable difference in the winter climate and amount of sunshine between Eastbourne and the Downs less than two miles away, though the difference in the level may be no more than 200 or 300 feet.

WEALD CLAY.

Within the area here dealt with there is a very small exposure of the Lower Cretaceous rocks, and they are entirely unfossiliferous.

The Weald Clay occupies an area of a quarter of a square mile at Langney, but no actual surface-section was visible. The formation was met with, however, in some experimental borings lately made by the Eastbourne Water Company, one within Sheet 334 being at the Pumping Station on the marsh north of Eastbourne. At this point a boring penetrated 201 feet into mottled red and grey clays without any sign of change. Though I washed and examined microscopically various samples of the clay, no fossils could be found, and we are still without any means of accurately estimating the thickness of this division. Mr. Whitaker thinks that the samples are more like lower than upper Weald Clay. The boring, though an entire failure from the point of view of water-supply, was of great scientific interest, and must be referred to more than once. I will, therefore, here give details of the strata passed through, from a record and samples communicated by Messrs. Le Grand & Sutcliff, my own notes being inserted in brackets :—

BORING AT EASTBOURNE.

		Thickness. Feet.	Depth. Feet.
[Alluvium, 30 feet].	Clay	5	5
	Peat	3	8
	Blue clay	22	30
[Upper Greensand, 35½ feet].	Green sand and clay [glauconitic]	29¼	59¼
	Sandstone [glauconitic]	¾	60
	Clay and a little sand [whitish and glauconitic]	2	62
	Sandstone [glauconitic]	3½	65½
[Gault, 286 feet].	Stony clay [hard, dark, sandy clay —junction beds ?]	2	67½
	Gault	171	238½
	Septarium	½	339
	Gault and fossils [*Inoceramus sulcatus*]	102½	341½
	Gault, green veins and fossils [*Ammonites lautus*]	10	351½

		Thickness. Feet.	Depth. Feet.
[Gault and Lower Greensand (?) 80½ feet].	Gault and sand [coarse, loamy sand, mixed black and green, at 360]	12	363½
	Sand [moderately coarse, with glauconitic grains, at 367]	3½	367
	Gault [clay] and sand [coarse sand and small phosphatic nodules with glauconitic grains at 400]	65	432
[Weald Clay, 201 feet].	Weald clay [light-grey sandy clay, at 432. Dark-grey clay at 436. Red-mottled clay to 510. Whitish silty clay, 6-inch seam, at 575. Red mottled clay at 586 (no change to bottom)]	201	633

Another boring, in Jevington parish but just beyond the limits of the Eastbourne map, penetrated 63 feet into Weald Clay of similar character.

LOWER GREENSAND.

Though, following the original survey, a small outcrop of Lower Greensand is shown on the map at Langney, it is by no means certain that the formation is represented near Eastbourne. West of Lewes, Lower Greensand is undoubtedly present, and several divisions can be traced in it; but eastward it seems to disappear, so that Gault rests either directly on Weald Clay, or is only separated from it by beds of sandy and gravelly clay, perhaps representing the Folkestone Beds. There has been a considerable amount of erosion between these formations, and this circumstance makes the thickness of the Weald Clay near Eastbourne still more difficult to estimate.

GAULT.

This formation occupies about a square mile of the area north of Eastbourne, and is also exposed on the foreshore between Eastbourne and Beachy Head. The ledges on the foreshore represent, however, only some 50 feet of the higher beds, the lower deposits north of Splash Point being hidden under the beach. No good inland sections are to be seen, though occasional excavations show Gault at St. Anthony's Hill, Horsey, and Hydneye. Our knowledge of the formation within the Eastbourne map must, therefore, be derived from the trial-boring at the Waterworks, and from the upper beds exposed on the greatly disturbed foreshore below high-water mark.

If the sandy clay coloured on the map as Lower Greensand is included, the total thickness of the Gault in the boring will be 366½ feet. Taking, however, the clay-bed with *Ammonites lautus* as the base, we reduce the thickness to 286 feet; but it should not be forgotten that *A. lautus* is a fossil usually found in a zone at some height up in the Gault, suggesting that part at least of the beds described by the well-sinker as "gault and sand" belong to the true Gault.

GEOLOGY OF EASTBOURNE.

The deposits seen on the foreshore consist of blackish sandy clays, sparingly fossiliferous but highly pyritised. They are brought in by a series of very curious overthrust faults, so that in at least one place Gault can be seen actually to overlie Lower Chalk. These disturbances will be again referred to (*see* p. 11).

UPPER GREENSAND.

The Gault passes upward into a thick bed of sand or sand-rock full of grains of glauconite and usually fossiliferous. This Upper Greensand is well exhibited at the base of the cliff and on the foreshore between Eastbourne and Beachy Head,* but is there very difficult to measure, owing to the numerous folds and sharp faults which coincide in direction with the coast-line. It should be observed also that the coast-section is deceptive, for, besides faulting, there is a sharp dip inland, which makes the strata appear much thinner than they really are. By piecing together the evidence collected on the coast from certain inland well-sections, I have obtained a probable thickness of 45 or 50 feet for this division. The Upper Greensand towards the top becomes lighter coloured, calcareous, fine-grained and hard, and contains scattered phosphatic nodules. In this condition it is very similar to the basal beds of the Chalk, which also contain scattered glauconitic grains. The exact boundary of the formation can only be ascertained by a reference to the fossils, though the sections of the junction-beds seen on the foreshore near Beachy Head are

FOSSILS OF THE UPPER GREENSAND.

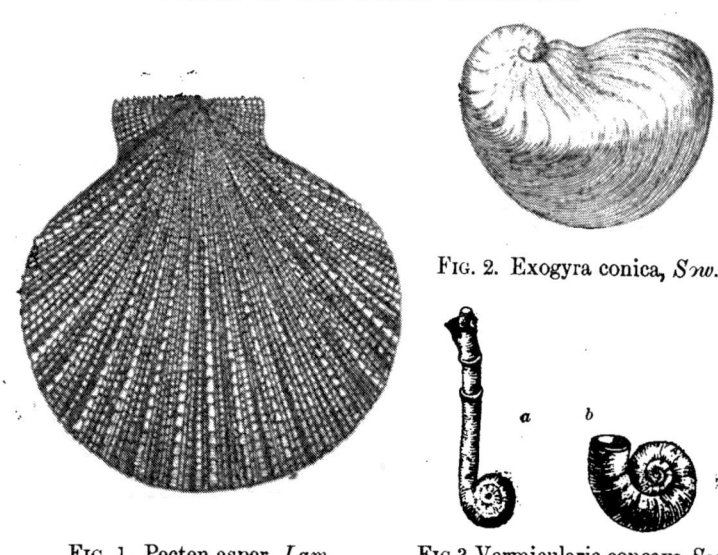

FIG. 1. Pecten asper, *Lam.* (⅔ natural size.)

FIG. 2. Exogyra conica, *Sow.*

FIG. 3. Vermicularia concava, *Sow.* (*b.* enlarged.)

---

* See also W. Topley, "Geology of the Weald." *Memoirs of the Geological Survey*, 1875, pp. 158, 159.

perfectly clear. Among the fossils of the Upper Greensand may be mentioned *Pecten asper* (Fig. 1), which, however, has not yet been recorded from Eastbourne, *Exogyra conica* (Fig. 2), and *Vermicularia concava* (Fig. 3). The green beds are also full of curious cylindrical cavities filled with material differing somewhat from the surrounding matrix. These are perhaps holes made by some boring animal, though the horizontal position and closed ends often suggest rather the disappearance of buried sand-eating holothurians.

CHALK

The Chalk, which occupies the greater part of the area of the Eastbourne Map, is about 900 feet in thickness, and has been divided into three well-marked groups of distinct lithological character. These are indicated on the map; but each group or stage is also divisible into zones, which are characterized by special assemblages of fossils. The zones recognizable in the Chalk of Sussex are as follow:—*

	Zones.
UPPER CHALK.—Soft white chalk, usually with bands of flint.	Belemnitella quadrata. Marsupites. Micraster coranguinum. ,, cortestudinarium.
(Chalk Rock) - - - -	Holaster planus.
MIDDLE CHALK.—Hard, rubbly white chalk, with a few flints near the top, and at the base a hard rock (Melbourne Rock)	Terebratulina gracilis. Rhynchonella Cuvieri.
LOWER CHALK.—Bedded marly grey Chalk. At the top soft marl (*Belemnitella* Marl); at the base hard flaggy beds with glauconite.	Belemnitella plena. Holaster subglobosus. Ammonites varians.

The Lower Chalk consists of well-bedded massive grey Chalk alternating with bands of softer marl, which in the disturbed cliff-section have been so squeezed out as to make the thickness of this division appear to be considerably less than inland measurements would indicate. Dr. Barrois† speaks of only 120 feet; but the true thickness is perhaps fully 180 feet. The lowest bed is hard and grey, with phosphatic nodules, fine sand and grains of glauconite. It contains many fossils, including *Nautilus lævigatus*, *Turrilites Morrisi*, *Avicula gryphœoides*, *Terebratula biplicata*, *Stauronema Carteri* and *Ammonites*

---

* Many fossils from the Chalk are figured in Dixon's "Geology of Sussex," 2nd edition, 4to, London, 1888.

† Recherches sur le Terrain Crétacé Supérieur le l'Angleterre et de l'Irlande. *Mem. Soc. Géol. du Nord*, Lille, 1876. See also note by the Rev. H. E. Maddock, published by A. J. Jukes-Browne, *Quart. Journ. Geol. Soc.*, Vol. xxxi., p 271; and F. G. Hilton Price, in Dixon's "Geology of Sussex," 2nd edition, p. 136, and W. Whitaker, *Geol. Mag.*, 1871, p. 198.

GEOLOGY OF EASTBOURNE

Fossils of the Lower Chalk.

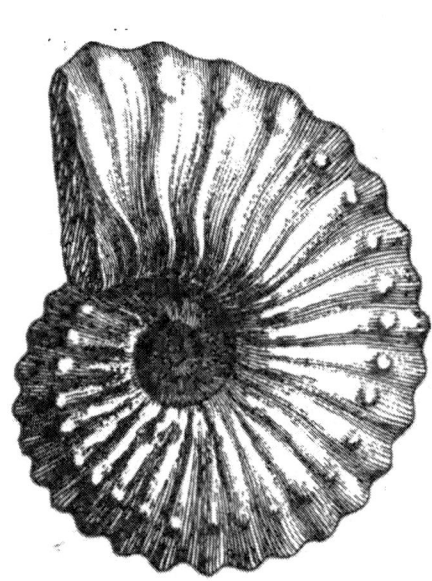

Fig. 4. Ammonites rotomagensis, *Brong.*
(Young specimen.)

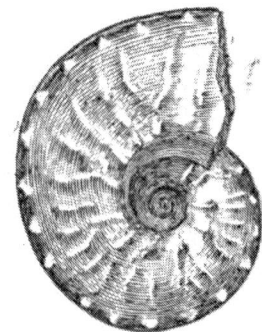

Fig. 5. Ammonites varians, *Sow.*
(⅔ natural size.)

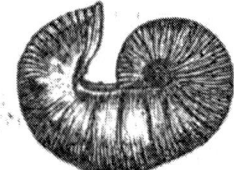

Fig. 6. Scaphites æqualis, *Sow.*

varians (Fig. 5), and is apparently equivalent to the Chloritic Marl of other districts. Next follow alternating hard and soft beds of grey marl, full of sponges in the lower part, and yielding *Ammonites rotomagensis* (Fig. 4), *Holaster subglobosus*, *Scaphites æqualis* (Fig. 6), and other fossils of the Chalk Marl. The top of the Lower Chalk consists of about 10 feet of soft grey marl containing *Belemnitella plena*. This marl is impervious, and can easily be found on the coast by the line of springs which are thrown out just above it, especially near Holywell.

The Middle Chalk consists of about 200 feet of hard rubbly white chalk with irregular partings of grey clay, and a few flints in the upper 50 feet. Towards the base it becomes still more indurated, and forms a hard rock—the "Melbourn Rock"—which can be followed as a distinct ledge for many miles along the face of the escarpment overlooking the Weald. The lower nodular beds are full of *Inoceramus mytiloides* (Fig. 10), and *Rhynchonella Cuvieri* (Fig. 11); above these come strata with *Echinoconus subrotundus* (Fig. 7), and *Terebratulina gracilis* (Fig. 8); at the top, or forming the base of the Upper Chalk, is the zone of *Holaster planus* (Fig. 9), equivalent to the Chalk Rock of other districts, and yielding the same peculiar fossils, though here no harder and no more conspicuous than the rest of the Chalk. It forms no recognizable feature in the escarpment.

Fossils of the Middle Chalk.

Fig. 7. Echinoconus subrotundus, *Mant*.

Fig. 8. Terebratulina gracilis, *Schloth*. (thrice natural size.)

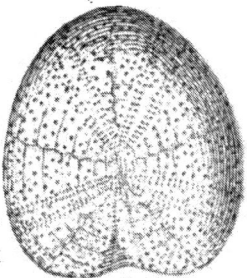

Fig. 9. Holaster planus, *Mant*.

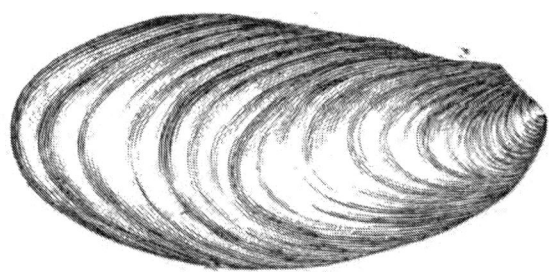

Fig. 10. Inoceramus mytiloides, *Mant*. (half natural size.)

Fig. 11. Rhynchonella Cuvieri, *d'Orb*. (twice natural size.)

The Upper Chalk is about 500 feet thick. It has been described by Dr. Barrois, but Mr. Jukes-Browne finds himself compelled to differ from that observer on some points, and the following account is by my colleague.

The lowest zone, that of *Micraster cortestudinarium*, is from 70 to 75 feet thick; near the base it contains some nodular layers, but the higher part consists of soft white chalk with many cavernous flints. The zone of *Micraster coranguinum* (Fig. 12) is much thicker than Dr. Barrois supposed; the lower 116 feet contains frequent layers of flints, both solid and cavernous, and at the top of this part is an indurated yellowish layer which Dr. Barrois regarded as identical with a similar layer at the base of the Marsupite zone near Margate. The chalk above, however, does not yield *Marsupites*, and contains many layers of flints for nearly 100 feet higher, and it is 138 feet before chalk with few flints is reached. The zone of *M. coranguinum* is certainly over 200 feet thick, and may be 254 feet. It occupies the greater part of the cliffs between Beachy Head and Cuckmere Haven; *Micraster coranguinum*, *Echinoconus conicus*, and *Rhynchonella plicatilis* (Fig. 14) are found in it.

Between this haven and Seaford the beds curve down to the west acquiring a dip of 8° or 10°. This brings in higher beds which consist of chalk with very few flints and with frequent seams of soft grey marl; these beds are about 50 feet thick and

FOSSILS OF THE UPPER CHALK.

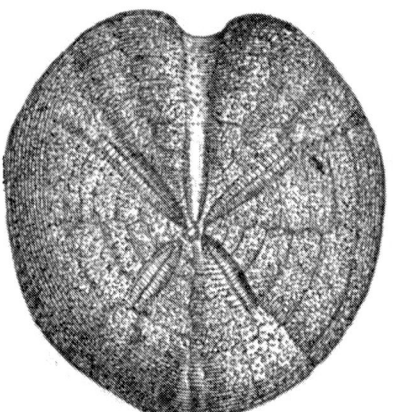

FIG. 12. Micraster coranguinum, *Lesk.*

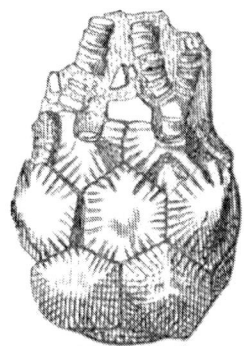

FIG. 13. Marsupites ornatus, *Miller.*

FIG. 14. Rhynchonella plicatilis (var. octoplicata), *Sow.*

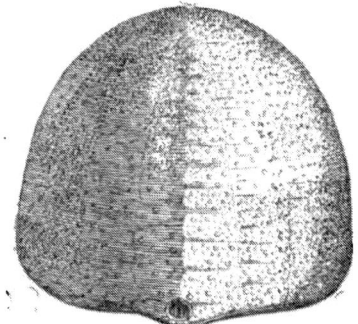

FIG. 15. Echinocorys vulgaris, *Breynius.* (¼ natural size.)

are believed to represent the zone of *Marsupites* (Fig. 13), though no plates of that fossil have yet been found at this locality in spite of careful search for them.

Above this in Seaford Cliff are about 130 feet of chalk containing layers of flints at intervals of 6 or 7 feet. This chalk contains *Offaster pillula* in some abundance, a species which seldom occurs below the zone of *Belemnitella quadrata*. This chalk is continued in the Newhaven Cliffs where *B. quadrata* has been found by Mr. Rhodes.

WOOLWICH BEDS AND LONDON CLAY.

Outliers of Woolwich Beds, capped in two places by a little London Clay, occur at Newhaven and Seaford. The sections are now obscure; but before the fort at Newhaven was made Prestwich and Mr. Whitaker were able to measure a clear exposure in the sea-cliff.

GEOLOGY OF EASTBOURNE

The following notes are condensed from their description*:—

Section of the cliff, Castle Hill, Newhaven.

		feet.
	Gravel	10
London Clay.	Grey clay Yellow sand Thin-bedded grey and brown clay Flint-pebbles in grey clay and yellow sand	13
Woolwich Beds, 60 feet or more.	Laminated grey-clay	4½
	Clayey, hard, oyster-bed	2
	Shelly clays	2
	Grey and brown clay, with bed of shells	2½
	Sand and seams of grey clay—traces of plants	6
	Grey clay, with leaves and shells Sandy bed with lignite	20 ?
	Grey, brown, and lilac clay	6
	Light-coloured sand	?
	Greensand, with green-coated and iron-stained flints Chalk with flints	2

From the shell-beds, Prestwich obtained the following species:—

Dreissena serrata ?
Unio.
Cyrena cuneiformis (fig. 17).
——— intermedia ?
Psammobia Condamini.
Hydrobia Parkinsoni ?
Cerithium variabile.
Melania inquinata (fig. 18).
Melanopsis buccinoides.
Ostrea Bellovacina (fig. 16).
Cypris ?

FOSSILS OF THE WOOLWICH BEDS.

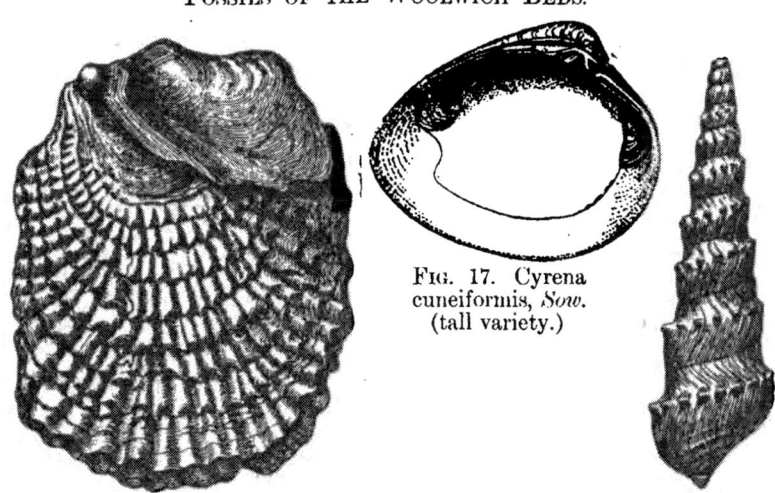

FIG. 16. Ostrea Bellovacina, *Lam.* (⅔ natural size.)

FIG. 17. Cyrena cuneiformis, *Sow.* (tall variety.)

FIG. 18. Melania inquinata, *Defr*

---

* Prestwich "On the Structure of the Strata between the London Clay and the Chalk in the London and Hampshire Tertiary Systems. Part II.—The Woolwich and Reading Series." *Quart. Journ. Geol. Soc.*, vol. x., pp. 83-84 (1854). Whitaker "On the Cliff-sections of the Tertiary Beds . . . at Newhaven in Sussex," *Ibid.*, vol. xxvii., pp. 265-268 (1871).

Dr. Mantell and Mr. Starkie Gardner have obtained also numerous leaves, but these have not yet been described.

The mollusca are estuarine forms, such as occur at Woolwich, and the strata also are of the Woolwich type. Towards the west these pass into deposits of the Reading type—red-mottled clays with lignite—as they do in the London Basin, and mollusca become very rare. The London Clay of Newhaven has yielded no fossils.

CLAY WITH FLINTS.

All the higher flat-topped Downs within the area here described are covered by a thin sheet of red or black clay, full of unworn flints or of Tertiary débris. This deposit is of indefinite date, being here formed principally from the gradual destruction of Eocene outliers, which have become mixed with a certain proportion of flints set loose by the slow dissolution of the Chalk below. It always contains a large percentage of rounded quartz grains, such as could not be derived from the Chalk below.

VALLEY GRAVEL OR COOMBE ROCK.

Eastbourne is built mainly on a deposit of Chalk rubble, like that known at Brighton as the Coombe Rock or Elephant-bed. This cannot now be examined, except in occasional excavations for foundations, but Prestwich describes it as yielding teeth and bones of *Elephas primigenius, Rhinoceros tichorhinus, Hippopotamus major, Bos* and *Equus*.* He was also told that at a mile east of Eastbourne "beneath the bone-bed they came, at a depth of 15 or 16 feet, upon a bed of sand with sea-shells." But "one mile east of Eastbourne" (Old) would mean a locality at the edge of the marsh, which was an estuary within the historic period. The marine beds, therefore, may be of modern date; but this point can only be cleared up by the opening of new pits. Should Prestwich's informant be correct, this is the only trace of Pleistocene marine deposits yet found within the Wealden area; though near Brighton a "raised beach" underlies the Coombe Rock.

At Birling Gap an excellent section of the Coombe Rock is exposed. It is fully 30 feet thick, and extends below mean tide-level. Up this valley, but not in the gravel, several Palæolithic implements have been found. Similar chalky rubble has been mapped in some of the dry Chalk valleys, as well as along the courses of the Ouse and Cuckmere.

ALLUVIUM AND SHINGLE.

The Alluvium of the Ouse and Cuckmere, and of the Willingdon Level, consists of carbonaceous mud and peat, which have gradually filled up valleys flooded on the subsidence of the land.

---

* "The Raised Beaches, and 'Head' or Rubble-drift, of the South of England. . . . ." *Quart. Journ. Geol. Soc.*, vol. xlviii., p. 366. (1892).

GEOLOGY OF EASTBOURNE.

The greater elevation of the land in old times is shown by the depth of the Alluvium, as proved by borings. Those made by the Newhaven Harbour Company prove that the Alluvium reaches in places at least 52 feet below the marsh-level, without any indication of solid rock. In other districts submerged land-surfaces, with tree-stumps rooted in the soil, are found beneath low-water level; but within the Eastbourne map there do not happen to be many deep excavations, though a trench at the Eastbourne Waterworks showed peat at about mean-tide level, and a total thickness of 30 feet of Alluvium. This submergence was apparently completed in prehistoric times.

Flints washed out of the Chalk have drifted along-shore to the north-east, and have accumulated north of Eastbourne in parallel ridges till they form a beach nearly a mile in width at Langney Point.* There is little beach along the rest of the coast, except at the mouth of the Ouse.

DISTURBANCES AND SURFACE EROSION.

The physical features are largely due to the disturbances which the rocks have undergone; but adequately to deal with the subject needs far more space than is here available. The general southward dip was caused by the rise of the main anticlinal fold of the Weald; to which also is due the shedding of the water, so that the rivers flow north or south from the central axis and cut across all the strata in succession. The Ouse and Cuckmere are two of these ancient rivers which have gradually cut lower and lower, till now they seem to have gone out of their way to cut through the high Chalk Downs, instead of following the easier and lower route across the plains of Gault or Weald Clay to the sea. The plains, however, at the time the river-valleys originated had no existence, or were higher than the present Chalk hills.†

The eastern extremity of the Hampshire Basin lies within the area described in this pamphlet, for the synclinal trough runs out to sea between Seaford and Beachy Head. This syncline is cut in a striking way by a disturbance which runs north-north-east and south-south-west along the shore from Eastbourne to Beachy Head. Part of this disturbance is shown on the map copied from the 6-inch survey; but it is traceable also through Eastbourne, till it is lost under the Marsh. The disturbance cuts at right angles to the general trend of the anticlinal and synclinal folds, and though lost beneath the sea near Beachy Head, it seems to continue in the same line, for the Admiralty charts mark a narrow shoal extending more than a mile further and suggesting the presence of a ledge of the green sandstone. The numerous minor disturbances which together make up this shattered belt consist in the main of small overthrust faults,

---

* See "Topley, Geology of the Weald," Chapter xvii., *Memoirs of the Geological Survey* (1875); J. B. Redman, Proc. Inst. Civ. Eng., vol. xi., p. 162; and F. W. Bourdillon, Rep. Brit. Assoc. for 1885, p. 413.

† Topley, *Op. cit.*, Chapter xvi.

12   GEOLOGY OF EASTBOURNE.

which cause Gault to overlie Greensand, and Greensand to rest on Chalk in a most unexpected fashion. Wedges have been so thrust in as to duplicate the rocks and give the strata a tilt

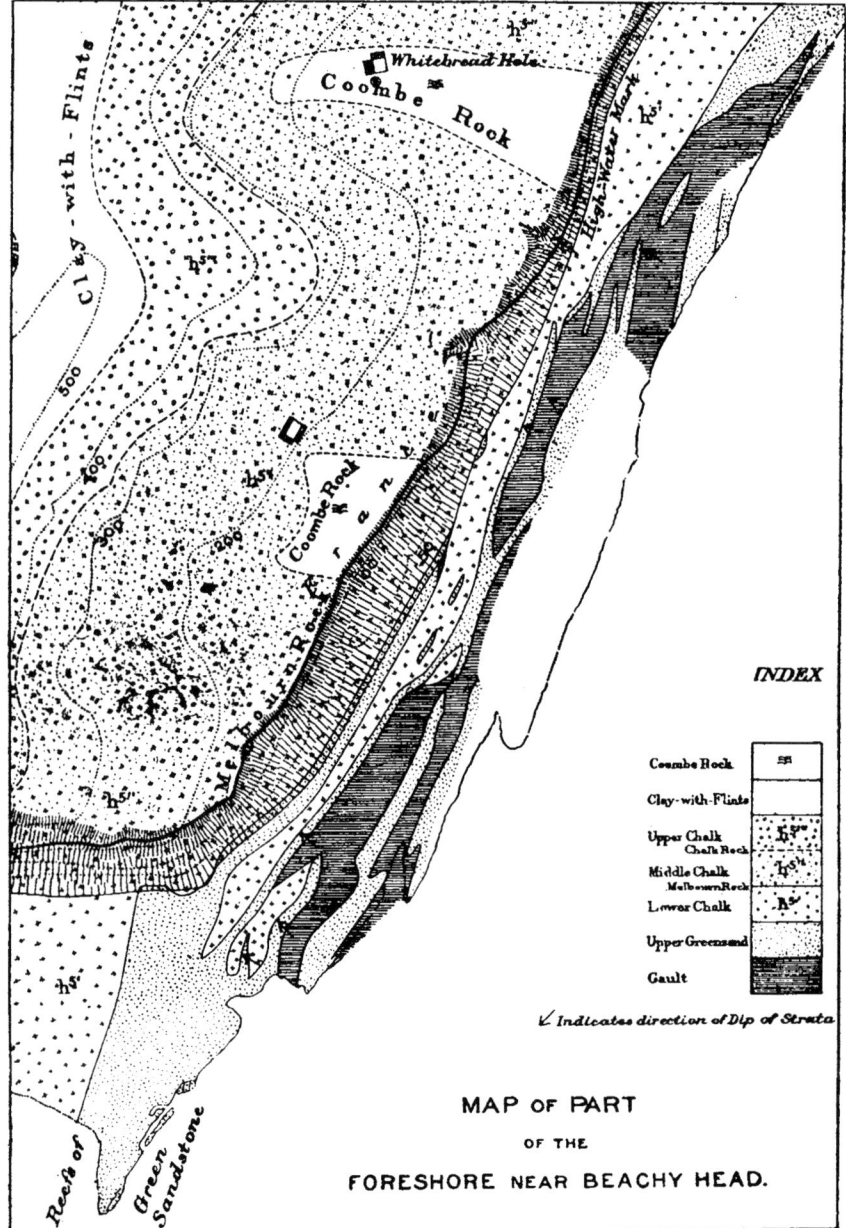

toward the west-north-west. The effect of this disturbance is only felt for a very short distance inland, but eastward under the sea it apparently becomes more violent, though without submarine surveying it is impossible to say exactly what has happened. The disturbance is probably a broken unicline, like that of the Isle of Wight, with which it may be continuous. If this is the case the Chalk of the South Downs, unlike that of the North Downs, is not connected across the Channel with France. Contrary to the accepted idea the escarpment curves round Beachy Head and turns to the west. The bed of this part of the English Channel may thus be a continuation of the wide plain of the Weald, and formed like the Weald by the erosion of the softer strata.

Another remarkable feature in the Eastbourne district is the occurrence in the Chalk Downs of numerous winding valleys, now quite devoid of water and having bottoms sloping at a much higher angle than that taken by the saturation-plane in the Chalk far beneath. Such a feature in pervious Chalk cannot be accounted for by any change in the amount of rainfall; it points to other conditions, which have now passed away. It is in all probability a relic of the Glacial Epoch, which in these southern districts did not lead to an accumulation of ice, but caused the rocks to freeze to a great depth, thus rendering them impervious to any rain that might fall in the summer. During that period the Chalk would be cut into valleys in the same way as any impervious rock, instead of immediately absorbing the heaviest rain, as it does at the present day.

Water Supply and Economics.

In a residential district of this character, water-supply is by far the most important practical application of geology. Eastbourne, till quite recently, obtained its water from headings driven into the Upper Greensand at the Bedford Well, north of the town, and obtained so large a supply as to make the source difficult to understand, for the outcrop of the Greensand is apparently of insufficient area to yield so much. A dry season and the consequent lowering of the water-level, by pumping caused, however, the influx of sea-water. The new Geological Survey shows that this well is in the remarkable disturbed belt which has just been described. This disturbance seems to have made itself felt in two ways. In the first place, by causing shattered Lower Chalk to abut against the Greensand, it let in a certain amount of water from the pervious Chalk above—a source which under ordinary conditions could not possibly be tapped by a well in the Greensand. The chemical analysis of the water and the unaccountably large supply obtained during a number of years support this view. Another result of the position of the well on the fissured belt was less fortunate, for it allowed sea-water to travel freely for a long distance and gradually to mix with the water of the well. As it was evident that other sources of supply were needed, the copious springs which formerly flowed into the sea at Holywell have now been taken, and wells have also been sunk at Wannock (north of the Eastbourne map) and at Friston. The latter of these localities is in the middle of sparsely inhabited Chalk Downs, and ought to yield a large supply of water of excellent quality. The following analyses of waters from these new sources have been made by Sir Edward Frankland :—

EASTBOURNE. Waterworks. March 20, 1897.

	Parts per 100,000.		
	(1) Holywell.	(2) Friston.	(3) Wannock.
Total Solid Matters	33·24	37·08	25·24
Organic Carbon	·055	·041	·043
Organic Nitrogen	·010	·012	·011
Ammonia	—	—	—
Nitrogen as Nitrates and Nitrites	·664	·656	·096
Total Combined Nitrogen	·674	·668	·107
Chlorine	5·2	4·3	2·6
Hardness Temporary	14·5	16·9	15·2
,, Permanent	7·3	7·0	4·2
,, Total	21·8	23·9	19·4

(1) is from base of Middle Chalk. (2) is from Upper Chalk. (3) is from shattered Lower Chalk.

"For Chalk waters they are all of moderate hardness, the Wannock Well remarkably so."

Seaford and Newhaven obtain their supply from wells in the Upper Chalk; but they also have been troubled by the influx of sea-water, and have been compelled to sink a new well further inland, at Poverty Bottom, in Denton.*

The mineral resources of the Eastbourne area are few. The Gault, or rather its superficial weathered layers, is dug for brickmaking at Horsey. The Upper Greensand yields a fairly hard sandstone, which was formerly taken from the reefs between tide marks and used for building-purposes. A good hydraulic lime is obtained from the marly Lower Chalk; and occasionally the harder beds have been employed for building, though they are too soft for anything but interior work. The Middle and Upper Chalk are more pure, and burn into a lime of ordinary character; they are also used for marling the land. The higher part of the Upper Chalk is so pure that it is dug at Newhaven.

---

* For further information, see Memoir on the Water Supply of Sussex, by W. Whitaker and C. Reid. (In the press.)

and shipped for use in chemical works. An analysis of this Chalk from Meeching Chalk Quarry, made by Mr. Bernard Dyer, gives :—

Carbonate of Lime	97·89
Phosphate of Lime	·22
Carbonate of Magnesia	·75
Oxide of Iron and Alumina	·14
Silica	·65
Water, &c.	·35
	100·00

In this pit the flints which are picked out are black and have very thin rinds; the proportion of flints is about 1 ton to 130 tons of chalk.

The Tertiary deposits yield sand and some brickearth, and also, at their junction with the Chalk, a hydrous aluminium sulphate, known as Aluminite or Websterite; but this mineral is of no economic value. The extensive beach at Langley Point yields flint gravel suitable for use in the manufacture of pottery; and certain parts of the alluvial mud of the Ouse can be used mixed with Chalk for cement-making.

Printed by Libri Plureos GmbH in Hamburg, Germany